"Chill the powder a
"Mix the batter quickly."
"Once time has passed, you can no longer use it."
"Fry in plenty of oil."

Please forget all this common sense

Tempura batter that never fails can be used by both those who have given up and those who are beginners.

cooking expert
Hiro's kitchen ♪

Over 25 years of research into home cooking

Winner of many recipe contests

Appeared on TV Published recipe book (textbook series)

YouTube channel with over 10,000 users

Lectured over 1000 people in online cooking class

Said to be an expert in solving cooking problems

Truly useful at home
I will share with you the techniques
that only a cookery researcher can

The recipes of professionals who run restaurants are really delicious. But if you try to make the same quality at home, there are some things you just can't copy, such as cooking utensils, quality of ingredients, and kitchen space.

That's when you need to turn to a "cookery expert.

Cookery experts do more than just come up with recipes; their job is to brush up professional techniques so that they can be used at home and improve the taste at home.

This book will introduce you to "Never-Fail Tempura".

There are no difficult techniques at all. We have tried many times so that anyone can succeed.

We hope you enjoy this unprecedented way of making tempura batter, which was born from a mix of professional techniques and home cooking experience.

~table of contents~

5 tips for making tempura without making mistakes

Recommended oil and tools for tempura

How to make tempura batter that will definitely fry crispy

basic tempura

- Shrimp · Chicken · Eggplant · Pumpkin · Sweet potato
- Various vegetable tempura (green pepper, lotus root, mushroom, perilla)

Make flowers bloom on tempura

basic kakiage

- Secret powder for crispy frying
- Kakiage that never fails
- Variations of kakiage

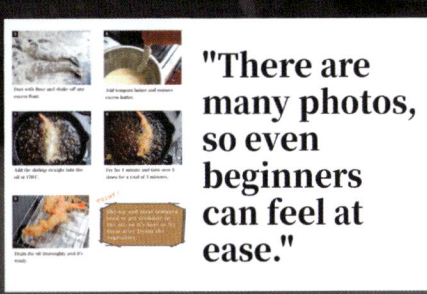

"There are many photos, so even beginners can feel at ease."

How to make delicious tempura sauce

- Tendon sauce that goes well with tempura
- How to make Tendon
- Arranged in Tentsuyu
- Recipes for salt that goes well with tempura

Q&A

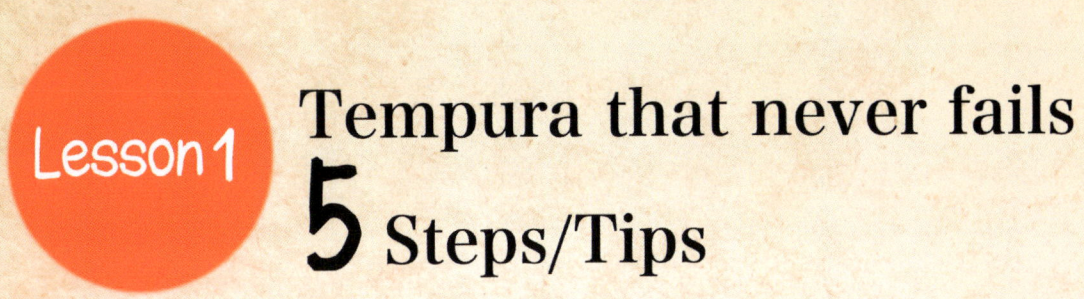

Lesson 1: Tempura that never fails — 5 Steps/Tips

1. Food Preparation

First, prepare the ingredients for "deep frying at 170-180°C for 3 minutes.

Cut hard vegetables into thin strips, shrimps into straight strips, eggplants into fan-shaped strips, and eggplants into uniform thickness.
The problem of tempura, "I don't know how much to fry," is solved by adjusting the size and shape of the ingredients. The recipe details how the ingredients can be "fried in 3 minutes in 170-180°C oil.

Next, we add "seasoning," the new standard for tempura.

Restaurants where the finest ingredients are available do not add seasoning. But that is not the case at home, is it? Therefore, we add seasoning to bring out the best flavor. This is how you can make tempura that is as good as restaurant tempura.

For example, eggplant is salted to remove water and scum, making it less likely to absorb oil and bringing out the best flavor. Salt the pumpkin to bring out the best of its sweetness. Chicken does not become tough when fried.

More details will be introduced in the chapter "Basic Tempura".

2. Never fail.
Prepare the tempura batter

The most important point of this recipe is to make the "never-fail tempura batter".

The cause of tempura failure is gluten. Gluten is a protein found in flour that becomes "sticky" when combined with water. When this "stickiness" is produced, the tempura absorbs oil and becomes sticky, causing it to fail.

Therefore, in order to prevent gluten from forming, restaurants make great efforts to serve delicious tempura, such as keeping the water cool, avoiding over-mixing, using the batter immediately after making it, covering the bowl with aluminum foil to protect it from heat, and discarding any leftover batter and making new ones.

It is very difficult to imitate them at home, isn't it?

So, this time, "Tempura Batter that Never Fails" uses "a method that does not generate gluten" with the knowledge of science. Science does not involve anything dangerous or difficult.

The only ingredients used for the batter are flour, water, and oil.

3. Uchiko(powdering)

Before battering the food, the ingredients are dredged in flour (a thin layer of flour).

There are many advantages to battering.

The batter is less likely to flake off.
The batter is evenly coated and looks delicious.
It also makes it easier for the batter to cook evenly.

However, it is not good to put a lot of batter.

If you put a lot of batter, the batter will absorb the oil and become heavy. The result is a failed tempura that makes you "full" after eating just one.

The goal is to spread the batter thinly over the entire ingredient. It sounds difficult, but anyone can succeed in batter by "putting thin flour on the ingredients and tapping it on and off. It is easy, so please try it.

The cause of most tempura failures at home is that the batter is not well controlled.

4. Deep-fry in oil at 170°C

Deep fry tempura in oil at 170-180°C.

Add a few drops of tempura batter and try to feel it drop down and come up quickly.

The temperature of the oil will change as the ingredients are added, so adjust the heat level. If it is difficult to adjust the heat, it is convenient to use the stove's automatic setting, so if it has a function, use it as much as possible.

If the oil temperature is lower than this, the tempura will be soggy. If the temperature is higher, the batter will be burnt and the food will not be cooked.

The key to avoiding failure is to fry in oil at 170-180°C.

The amount of oil you want to use is just enough to float the ingredients you want to fry. However, if you're using tempura batter that never fails, you don't have to worry about the amount of oil that much.

If you don't want to use a lot of oil, prepare a small, deep pot. Provides sufficient depth.

We will introduce in detail what kind of pot we recommend on the tempura tools page.

5. Cut oil thoroughly.

When you are done frying tempura, drain the oil while it is "floating".

Tempura absorbs more oil than expected. Placing it on a net will drain the oil well. When the oil is drained, the tempura will be light and crispy texture will last longer.

You can also use paper to drain oil, but the paper will absorb steam and the tempura will steam and the texture will deteriorate.

extra point

Remove tenkasu (Tempura batter pieces) frequently.
If tempura is fried one after another with tenkasu remaining, the tenkasu will be burnt and the oil will be damaged quickly.

Frying Tempura
Recommended oil

You can use any "cooking oil" to fry tempura.

Using "oil suitable for tempura" will make it even lighter and crispier, making it easier to eat. The following oils are recommended.

Sesame oil
Rice oil
Canola oil (rapeseed oil)
Olive oil

These oils are high in oleic acid and resistant to heat. Compared to tempura fried in common salad oil, the texture is lighter and less upsetting to the stomach, and you can eat as much as you like.

But they are expensive.

So here is a recommended method.

Salad oil 3: Recommended oil 1 This is a mixture of the two.

This will make tempura more crispy while keeping the price down.

When frying tempura Tools to use

Smaller pans are easier to fry.

A frying pan of about 22cm is perfect for frying tempura. (For about 4 people)
If you use a smaller, deeper pot, you can get more depth with less oil, making it easier to use when frying a small number of people.

Tongs are recommended.

Chopsticks are recommended for adding tempura batter, while tongs are recommended for flipping and grabbing tempura. Since tongs have a larger surface area to hold the batter, the batter is less likely to fall apart, reducing mistakes.

To drain oil well

Prepare a mesh bat to drain the tempura oil. If you drain the oil while it is floating, the crispiness will last longer, and you can put it directly into the oven when you reheat.

A more tasty touch!

Prepare a net or a scoop for scooping out the tenkasu.
A 100-yen store item will suffice.

*Please be careful when using shallow and small pots or frying pans, as fire can easily enter from the side and catch fire.
*No matter what utensils you use, keep an eye on them while frying.

The secret to never failing is "science.

Crispy tempura batter

The power of science makes it easy

You can make crispy, delicious tempura at home. It is really easy to make. The secret is to mix the flour and oil first, which coats the flour with oil and prevents gluten from forming. You will be surprised to know that this tempura batter can be fried crispy and delicious even if it is not cooled, mixed thoroughly, or left at room temperature for a long time.

Ingredients 2 servings

weak flour … 60g
oil … 30g
water … 90〜105ml

*Lower amounts of water will result in a firm batter that is less likely to fail. More water will result in a thin, luxurious tempura batter.

Hint: "cookies."

Actually, I discovered this tempura batter from the way cookies are made.
To make cookies crispy, butter is mixed with flour before baking. I thought, "Couldn't this be used for tempura?" So I researched the amounts and perfected it.

Only 3 ingredients are needed! Any kind of oil is OK!

Lesson 4
Never fail!
How to make tempura batter

*Use a scale to measure.

1 measure flour

Measure out 30 grams of flour per person.

Be sure to use light flour for a crispy batter.
If it does not say so on the bag, look at the ingredient list and choose one with less than 9 grams of protein in 100 grams of flour.

2 mix up oil

Add half the weight of oil as flour.
(e.g. 30g flour:15g oil)
Mix until the whole mixture becomes thick.

Mix thoroughly until there is no powdery residue.

3 mix water with water

Add 1.5 to 1.8 times the amount of water as flour.
(90-105 ml water) Mix until the whole mixture is thickened. The recommended amount of water is 1.7 times the amount of flour.

It is okay to mix thoroughly.

Making standard ingredients more delicious

Basic Tempura

With a little ingenuity Restaurant Quality

Preparing the ingredients is very important for tempura.
The more preparation you do, the better the tempura will taste. Even if you make a slight mistake in frying, as long as the ingredients are well prepared, the effect is that you can recover to a level where the mistake is not noticeable.

Easy once you get used to it

The tempura batter I mentioned earlier can be made by eye once you get used to it. Put the flour into a bowl and add oil while stirring to thicken. Add water a little at a time until the desired thickness is reached, and the tempura batter is ready.
Now you can easily make "I want to deep fry a little for dinner," "I want to put a little tempura in my lunch box," or "I want to deep fry only this ingredient.

Crunchy after a period of time

The never-fail tempura batter is crispy even an hour after frying. It tastes great even when cold, so it is recommended for bento lunches.

*Prepare an appropriate amount of oil for frying.
*All ingredients are for 2 servings.
*The amount of water for the tempura batter is 1.7 times the amount of flour.
*Guideline for the amount of tempura batter is given in each recipe. Please make and prepare the tempura batter before preparing the ingredients.

"Let's make it from shrimp tempura!"

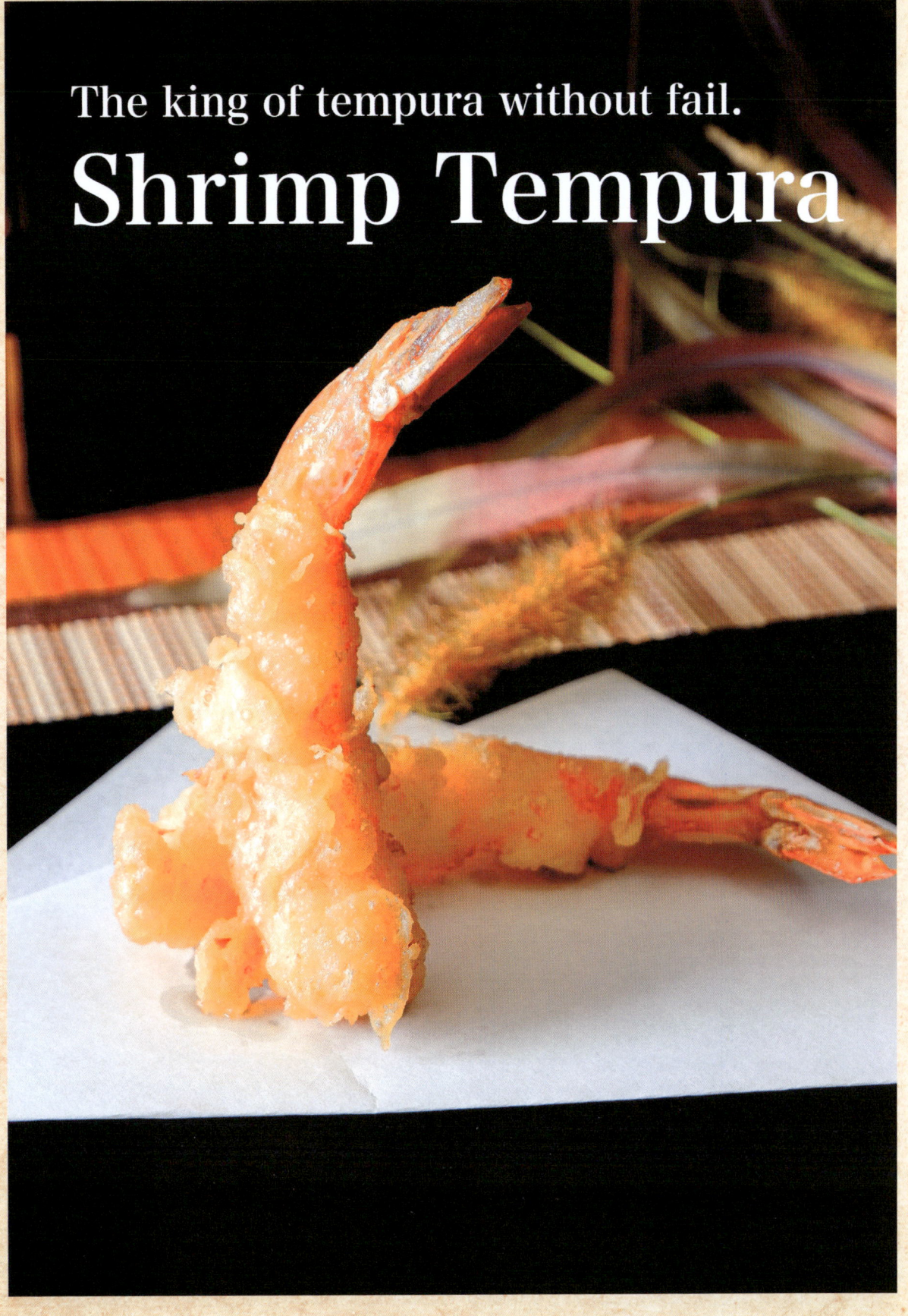

ingredient

Shrimp......4
Flour………30g
Oil…………15g
Water………50ml
Battering powder …as needed

Deep fry "Shrimp," the king of tempura, without fail.

There are two important points in shrimp preparation.
1) Cut off the tip of the tail to prevent explosion.
2) Fold the meat to make it straight.

If you do this, you will not fail. The shrimp can be deep-fried in oil at 170℃ for 2 to 3 minutes. Enjoy the "plump" texture.

Peel the shell and legs, leaving the tail intact.

Cut the tip and center of the tail diagonally and let the water drain out.

Make 3 incisions on the belly side of the shrimp. Approximately 1/3 the thickness of the shrimp

Fold the shrimp back and straighten it to avoid tearing it.

Dust with flour and shake off any excess flour.

Add tempura batter and remove excess batter.

Add the shrimp straight into the oil at 170°C.

Fry for 1 minute and turn over 3 times for a total of 3 minutes.

Drain the oil thoroughly and it's ready.

POINT!

Shrimp and meat tempura tend to get aromatic in the oil, so it's best to fry them after frying the vegetables.

The removed shrimp heads, shells, and legs are slowly fried in oil at 170℃ until crispy, making natural shrimp crackers. I love it.

Eggplant tempura
The secret to juicy but not oily is "salt"

ingredient

Eggplant......2
Salt.........1g (a pinch)
30g flour
Oil.........15g
Water.........50ml
Flour...as needed

Eggplant is one of the most difficult vegetables to prepare for tempura because it absorbs oil easily and is thick. So, it can be fried without failure by spreading it out like a fan (chasen cut) and adjusting the thickness. It is also tasty sliced in rounds or in pieces, so you can prepare it as you like. Also, sprinkle the eggplant with salt to remove the water that makes the eggplant acrid. This will enhance the sweetness of the eggplant and prevent it from absorbing oil.

Cut the stem of the eggplant and cut it lengthwise into 4 equal pieces.

Make 3 vertical incisions leaving 1 cm on the thin end and press lightly to shape.

Sprinkle salt on the cut eggplant and tap it with your fingers to coat it.

Leave it on for about 10 minutes and wipe off any water that comes out.

For round slices, cut into 1cm thick pieces.

Dust with flour to remove excess powder.

Dip in tempura batter and remove excess batter.

Place skin side down in oil at 170°C. Fry for 1 minute and turn over 3 times for a total of 3 minutes.

The best time is when the entire area is slightly colored.

Drain off the oil thoroughly and it is ready to serve.

POINT!

Salted eggplant can be enjoyed even by those who do not like eggplant. But if you want to enjoy the juicy texture and blue flavor typical of eggplant, skip steps 3 and 4.

``Tempura Shikigami'' has a luxurious feel, which is nice. It looks more stylish than kitchen paper. By the way, it is sold for 100 yen.

ingredient

Chicken breast......1 (about 300g)
Salt............1.5g
Sugar.........1g
1 teaspoon soy sauce
1/2 teaspoon garlic, grated
Flour......30g
Oil............15g
Water............50ml
Flour......Additional amount

Let's deep-fry juicy Kashiwa-ten (chicken breast tempura), which is popular in the Kansai region and around the world. Chicken breast has a strong flavor, but you may be concerned about its "dryness. So, we season them with salt and sugar, a professional technique. This is the only way to make them juicy and tender.

Remove the skin from the chicken breast.

Cut into 5 mm-thick shavings.

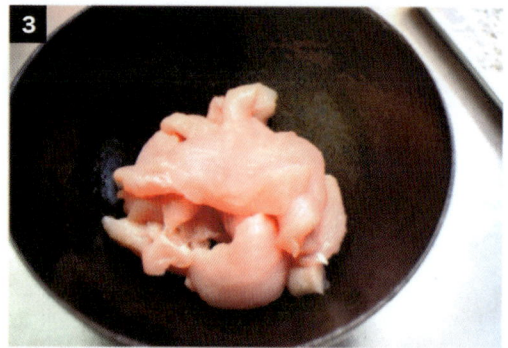

Rub salt and sugar well and let stand for 10 minutes.

Salt and sugar retain water in the chicken breast.

After 10 minutes, lightly rub in garlic and soy sauce.

Coat the chicken breast with flour and remove excess flour.

Dip in tempura batter and remove excess batter.

Place in oil at 170°C. Fry for 1 minute and turn over 3 times for a total of 3 minutes.

The best frying time is when the soy sauce used for the seasoning is slightly burnt.

Drain off the oil thoroughly and it is ready to serve.

It is so juicy that it is hard to believe it is chicken breast. I prefer it to shrimp tempura because the garlic and soy sauce flavor makes the rice go faster.

chef's voice

The oil after frying the shrimp and meat has a delicious flavor. If you make tenkasu with this oil, you can enjoy a higher-grade taste.

Natural sweetness brought out.
Tempura sweet potato Pumpkin

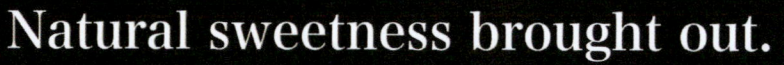

Ingredients
sweet potato or pumpkin ...4 slices
Light flour.........30g
Oil....................15g
Water...............50ml
Pinch of salt
A little flour

Here's how to enhance the ho-hum sweetness of sweet potatoes and pumpkins. The secret is salt. It is only a pinch, but when you let the ingredients get used to it, the excess moisture is removed and the sweetness is enhanced. Tempura is a dish that does not require seasoning, but I season it to make it tasty.

Slice into 5 mm slices.

Lightly rub salt on both sides and let stand for 10 minutes.

Flour the sweet potatoes and remove excess flour.

Dip in tempura batter and remove excess batter.

Place in oil at 170°C and deep fry for 1 minute. Turn over and fry for 1 minute, then return and fry for 1 minute.

Fry for a total of 3 minutes and you are done.

Drain oil thoroughly.

Deep fry pumpkin in the same procedure.

POINT !

Take the time to drain the oil thoroughly. While the oil is draining, the residual heat turns the starch into sugar, making it even sweeter and firmer.

Actually, I'm not good at making tempura. I thought, ``I really want to be good at making it!'' and after five years of research, I finally completed this batter.

Various vegetable tempura

*Every recipe can be made with the same amount of tempura batter.

Flour.........30g
Oil...............15g
Water...............50ml
Battering flour......Adequate amount

Tempura of green pepper

3 green peppers...... medium

1) Cut peppers in half and remove seeds and heads.
2) Dredge peppers in flour and tempura batter, removing excess flour.
3) Fry in oil at 170°C for 2 to 3 minutes, turning 3 times.

lotus root tempura

lotus root......150g

1) Peel lotus root and cut into 1cm thick half-moon slices.
2) Coat the lotus root with flour and tempura batter and remove excess flour.
3) Deep fry in oil at 170°C for 3 minutes, turning 3 times, then drain off the oil.

Tempura of Mushroom

Mushrooms..... .2 pcs.

1) Cut off the stones from the mushrooms and cut them in half.
2) Coat the mushrooms with flour and tempura batter and remove excess flour.
3) Deep fry in oil at 170°C for 3 minutes, turning 3 times.

Tempura of shiso leaves

shiso leaves······4

1) Dust the back of the shiso leaves with flour.
2) Put the tempura batter on the back of the shiso leaves only, and put them in oil at 170°C, batter side down.
3) Deep fry for 30 seconds, turn over and deep fry for 15 seconds, then drain off the oil.

How to make tempura flowers bloom

This will thicken the tempura batter and give it a crispy texture.

Put the tempura ingredients into the oil at 170°C.

Fry for about 1 minute until the batter has set, then sprinkle two spoonfuls of tempura batter on top.

Lightly tap the tempura ingredients to spread the batter.

Gather the spread batter and attach it to the tempura ingredients.

Drain the oil thoroughly and it's ready.

The way to make tempura bloom is to make lots of dregs. Remove the dregs frequently.

The method of making flowers bloom can be used with any ingredients.

Switch to potato starch and you won't fail!

basic kakiage

Ingredients for 2 people

onion	…	1/4
Carrot	…	1/5
mitsuba	…	1/2
potato starch	…	1 tablespoon
cake flour	…	50g
oil	…	25g
water	…	85ml

*The water for the tempura batter is made with 1.7 times the amount of soft flour.

Solve your kakiage failure with potato starch

For the tempura I made earlier, I used soft flour, but since kakiage tends to get sticky, I use potato starch.
This is because potato starch gives a crispier texture than soft flour. You can use rice flour instead of potato starch.

Easy to use in a small, deep pot

If you want to fry kakiage into perfectly round pieces, use a small, deep pot.
If you add the kakiage seeds in pieces, they will fry to just the size of the pot. Now anyone can make beautiful round kakiage without any technical skills.

Bite size is good

Making large kakiage at home is difficult. The recommended method is ``thin kakiage.''
The kakiage, scooped twice with a fork, is the perfect size for everyday side dishes and lunch boxes.
Thin kakiage will fry better in shallow oil, so it's very useful when you just want to make something.

2-3 types are best

If you add too many ingredients to kakiage, the flavor will become dull and boring. You can enjoy individuality by frying with 2 to 3 types of ingredients. Try adding more variations by using your favorite ingredients.

Cut the onions and carrots into strips of equal thickness.

The thickness is about 2mm

Cut the mitsuba leaves into 3cm pieces.

Place the vegetables in a bowl and coat with potato starch.

Mix flour with oil and water to make tempura batter.

Mix well with the tempura batter. It's good if you feel like there's a lot of clothing on it.

Heat the oil to 170°C and scoop the seeds with a fork in two batches.

Fry for 1 minute and flip.
*Don't touch it until you turn it over! It will fall apart.

Wait 1 minute, turn it over again, fry for another 1 minute, and it's done.

Set the kakiage up and drain the oil thoroughly.

POINT!

Aim for the thickness of the kakiage to be 1 to 2 cm. If you want to make a large kakiage, you can make it without making mistakes by making it ``large on the side''.

chef's voice

If you add it with a fork, excess tempura batter will fall off, making it easier to fry crispy.

Enjoy by changing
the ingredients and cutting methods.
various kakiage

[Basic frying method]

① Add 1 tablespoon of potato starch to the ingredients.
② Toss with tempura batter
③ Put it into the oil with a fork.
④ Fry in oil at 170°C for 1 minute, turn over repeatedly, and fry for 3 minutes.
⑤ Stand it upright and drain the oil.

*The amount of tempura batter used is the same for all recipes.

Light flour…50g
Oil…………25g
Water……85ml
Flour…appropriate amount

Onion...1/2 piece
Red ginger...3 pinches

① Cut the onion into strips along the fibers.
② Mix onions and pickled ginger
③ Fry using the basic frying method

onion and red ginger kakiage

Edamame and crab sticks kakiage

Edamame······100g with skin still on
Crab stick······50g

① Remove the edamame from the pods
② Cut the crab sticks into 1cm cubes.
③ Mix the edamame and crab sticks.
④ Fry using the basic frying method

potatoes and bacon kakiage

Potatoes...100g
Bacon...50g
Pepper......a little

① Peel the potatoes and cut them into 1cm cubes
② Cut the bacon into 1cm cubes.
③ Mix potatoes and bacon.
④ Fry using the basic frying method

Corn (grains)...100g
Wiener...2 pieces

① Cut the sausage into 1cm thick pieces.
② Mix the corn and sausage.
③ Fry using the basic frying method

corn and wiener kakiage

Make tempura more delicious
Tendon sauce, tentsuyu, salt

Tendon sauce is easy

Tendon sauce is very easy to make. The only ingredients are soy sauce, sugar, and mirin. Boil it in a ratio of 4:1:1 and it's done.
This tempura sauce will last for about 2 months in the refrigerator, so you can use it to season stews, add it to hamburgers, and make it into a Japanese-style sauce.

The different salt is also delicious.

I like tempura soup, but I also love salt, which makes the batter crispy.
It's delicious just sprinkled with rock salt or sea salt, but it's also fun to change the flavor of the salt.
Just add matcha, curry powder, or mix in the remaining spices and herbs in the refrigerator to create delicious ``changed salt.''

Tentsuyu with Tendon sauce

You can easily make tempura soup by diluting the tempura sauce with dashi stock.
If you don't have stock, you can make a delicious tempura soup without stock by diluting the tempura sauce with hot water and adding a pinch of bonito flakes.

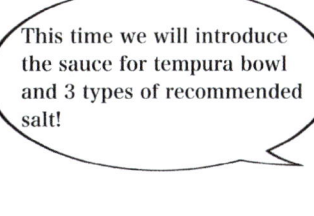

This time we will introduce the sauce for tempura bowl and 3 types of recommended salt!

Tendon sauce

Ingredients
Soy sauce……4 tablespoons
Sugar…………1 tablespoon
Mirin…………1 tablespoon

Add sugar and mirin to the pot.

Bring to a boil to evaporate the alcohol.

Add soy sauce and heat until bubbling around the edges of the pot.

Turn off the heat, dissolve the sugar well and put it in a storage container.

*What can be used in place of mirin

For white wine…..2 tablespoons
For sake……………2 tablespoons
For sugar:…………1/2 tablespoon

POINT!

If using white wine or sake, boil it down until it reduces by half in step 2. Then add soy sauce.

How to make Tendon

① Place the rice in a bowl and sprinkle with the tempura sauce (appropriate amount).
② Arrange your favorite tempura/kakiage on the plate.
③ To finish, sprinkle the tempura sauce over once and it's done.
POINT!
Tendon is more delicious when the tempura is coated in a thicker batter (with flowers in bloom).

How to make tentsuyu

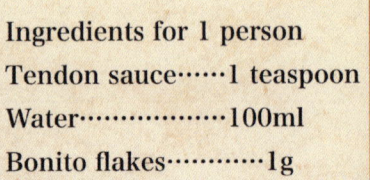

Ingredients for 1 person
Tendon sauce……1 teaspoon
Water……………100ml
Bonito flakes…………1g

Heat the water and bring it to a boil.

Add the bonito flakes and turn off the heat. The soup stock is now complete.

Pour the tempura sauce into a bowl, making sure not to add the bonito flakes, and the tempura sauce is complete.

[Easy version]
Place the tempura sauce and bonito flakes in a bowl and pour hot water over. This will also make a delicious tempura sauce.

It's also delicious with grated ginger and grated daikon radish.

``Salt" that brings out the deliciousness

- Curry powder + salt   It goes well with fish and meat.

- Herb + salt   This time I mixed basil. It goes well with tempura fried in olive oil.

- Cumin + salt   Ethnic scents and vegetables go well together, so it's perfect when you're tired of Japanese food.

Try adding any spices or herbs you have left at home (black pepper, oregano, allspice, etc.) to the salt. You can adjust the amount according to your preference, you can't go wrong.

Read this when you are having trouble making tempura.

Q&A

Will adding oil to the batter make it heavier?

The oil added to the tempura batter will come out during frying. Tempura batter, which never fails, gives a lighter result than regular tempura.

Please tell me how to reheat tempura in a delicious way.

We recommend heating it in an oven at 120°C for 5 to 10 minutes. Alternatively, you can warm it up in a toaster or fish grill on low heat, taking care not to burn it.

How many days does oil last?

It is best to use new oil every time. However, it is expensive, so I change it after frying it for about 3 times for 4 people.

How long does tempura batter last?

The finished tempura batter can be stored in the refrigerator for about half a day. It is very easy to use when meal times are different.

How should I adjust the temperature of the oil?

If you don't have a temperature control function, drop a few drops of batter into an open area of the pot and see how it goes.
The temperature of the oil is high if it spreads as soon as you put it in, and it's low if it doesn't float forever. The perfect temperature (170°C) is when it sinks momentarily and then rises immediately. If you check it frequently, you can reduce the chances of failure.

Are there any recommended ingredients that are not written in the book?

Basically anything you fry is delicious. Okra, zucchini, burdock, wild vegetables, chicken thighs, pork, etc. can all be fried deliciously. My recommendation is mushrooms. Shiitake mushrooms, maitake mushrooms, and perhaps surprisingly, nameko mushrooms are delicious when made into tempura.

What should I do with the Tenkasu I made?

Tenkasu can be stored in the refrigerator for one week. You can use it for okonomiyaki or takoyaki, make an ``easy tempura bowl" by putting chopped green onions and tempura on top of rice and pouring tempura sauce over it, or pour a little bit into miso soup to give it a richer flavor...try it out in a variety of ways.

"Thank You for Mastering Tempura with Us!"

Wow, you made it to the end—thank you so much for choosing Foolproof Tempura Mastery! We're beyond thrilled to have been part of your journey to discovering the joy of tempura.

With this book, you're now ready to turn any ingredient—shrimp, veggies, you name it—into perfectly crispy, light, and delicious tempura. No more worrying about soggy or heavy results! We hope you're feeling confident and excited to enjoy tempura anytime you want.

If you found this book helpful, loved a recipe, or just had fun trying something new, we'd be so grateful if you could share your thoughts in a quick review.
Your honest feedback means the world to us—and it can be a game-changer for others who are curious about tempura but hesitant to try. Your words might inspire someone else to create their own crispy masterpiece and bring a smile to their kitchen!

It only takes a minute: just drop a star rating and a line or two about what you loved or how it worked for you.
Together, let's spread the love for tempura across America!

YouTube channel
https://youtube.com/@cookingclasshiro4688?si=VwkB9Nn8UZFZNe87

blog
https://hirosankitchen.com/

online cooking class
https://www.street-academy.com/steachers/546788

Printed in Dunstable, United Kingdom